melanie walsh

my green day

10 green things I can do today

CANDLEWICK PRESS

Good morning! When I wake up . . .

I eat a free-range egg for breakfast.

Hens that have access to the outdoors instead of being kept in cages have more space to live in and are able to walk, spread their wings, and lay eggs in nests, all important natural behaviors.

I put my eggshell
in the compost bin . . .

Some household waste is biodegradable. Composting it means that less garbage goes to landfills.

where it will turn into
soil for growing vegetables.

I help empty the washing machine . . .

A tumble dryer is more energy-intensive than any other household appliance. Drying clothes on a line uses only free natural energy.

and hang our clothes out to dry.

At school . . .

I make presents
for my grandma.

Making art and toys out of old materials is fun and a great way to recycle.

At lunch . . .

I eat up all my pasta.

We throw away one third of all the food we buy. If we bought only the food we actually needed to eat, we wouldn't have to grow or transport so much food, which would save lots of energy.

After school, Mommy
and I go to the store . . .

and use our own bags
to pack the groceries.

Cloth bags can be used again and again. You'll never need to use another plastic bag.

In the park . . .

I play hide-and-seek
in the trees.

Playing outside with friends keeps you fit and makes you feel good.

flour

PUMPKIN SEEDS

HONEY

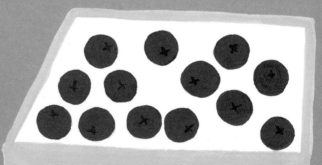

Then Daddy and I bake . . .

my yummy cookbook

delicious muffins for snacktime.

Homemade food doesn't need to contain extra ingredients such as food coloring and preservatives, so it is better for you than packaged foods.

Store-bought food is also often heavily packaged, which is a source of unnecessary waste.

In the evening . . .

You can save money and energy by keeping your household heating set low.

I put on a sweater
when I get chilly.

I have a shower before I go to bed . . .

You can reduce the amount of water you use by showering for only three or four minutes.

and that's the end of
my green day.